Cool
SCHOOL
MUSIC

Karen Latchana Kenney

A Division of ABDO

ABDO
Publishing Company

visit us at www.abdopublishing.com

Published by ABDO Publishing Company, a division of ABDO, P.O. Box 398166, Minneapolis, Minnesota 55439. Copyright © 2011 by Abdo Consulting Group, Inc. International copyrights reserved in all countries. No part of this book may be reproduced in any form without written permission from the publisher. Checkerboard Library™ is a trademark and logo of ABDO Publishing Company.

Printed in the United States of America, North Mankato, Minnesota
112010
012011

 PRINTED ON RECYCLED PAPER

Editor: Liz Salzmann
Series Concept: Nancy Tuminelly
Cover and Interior Design: Anders Hanson, Mighty Media, Inc.
Photo Credits: Anders Hanson, Shutterstock, Thinkstock

The following manufacturers/names appearing in this book are trademarks:
Aleen's® Tacky Glue®, Clean Colors® Rich Art®, Elmer's® Glue-All™

Library of Congress Cataloging-in-Publication Data

Kenney, Karen Latchana.
 Cool school music : fun ideas and activities to build school spirit / Karen Latchana Kenney.
    p. cm. -- (Cool school spirit)
 Includes bibliographical references and index.
 ISBN 978-1-61714-669-5
 1. School music--Instruction and study--Juvenile literature. 2. School music--Instruction and study--Activity programs--Juvenile literature. I. Title.
 MT930.K37 2011
 372.87--dc22
                              2010024874

Contents

What's Cool About School Music?

Going to school is not just about homework and tests. You get to meet new friends and learn amazing new things. Plus, there are so many activities to do and fun groups to join.

Being excited about school is your school spirit. One way to show it is by joining a school group. What do you love doing? Can you dance or sing? Or do you like to play games or learn languages? Guess what? School groups are filled with other students who like doing the same things as you!

Music groups are really cool to join! Do you like listening to music? It's just as fun to *make* music. You can use instruments or your voice to make music in groups. Doesn't that sound fun? If you want to show school spirit, school music may be right for you!

4

Before You Start

It's a good idea to do some research before joining a group. Talk to music group members. Go to a few **concerts** and watch their **rehearsals**. See if the group is what you *want* to join and *can* join.

Time

➤ How often does the group meet?

➤ How long are rehearsals?

➤ Are there any trips required?

➤ How many hours do you need to practice each week?

Skills

➤ What do members do at rehearsals?

➤ Do I need to know how to play an instrument or sing?

➤ How do I join the group?

Cost

➤ Do I need to pay a group fee?

➤ How much do instruments cost?

➤ Do I need to buy a uniform?

Permission

Once you've done your research, check it out with your parents. Make sure you get permission to join the group. You may need a parent's help to fill out an application or registration form.

The World of School Music

Do you have a good ear for music? You should try creating music! There are lots of music groups to join at school. Here are a few choices.

If you like singing, a choir or glee club may be the perfect choice for you. Choirs sing longer songs, while glee clubs sing shorter songs.

Singing groups are divided into parts. The lowest parts are bass parts. The highest parts are soprano parts. The parts in between are tenor and alto. The group sings their parts of a song together in harmony.

If you want to learn an instrument, you should join band or **orchestra**. There are many different instruments including violin, flute, guitar, and drums.

After hours of practice, music groups get to perform their songs. Performances are a really fun part of school music. Most groups put on **concerts** for students or parents. Pep and marching bands perform at school games and pep rallies.

Being part of a music group is a great experience. See what music groups your school has to offer. The right group is waiting for you!

Way Back

The oldest glee club in America is the Harvard Glee Club. It was started in 1858 as an all-male group. They sang European and American college songs. They also sang popular show tunes and folk songs. The club still exists today and sings all over the world.

Tools & Supplies

Here are some of the materials you'll need to make the projects in this book!

index cards

magazines

paper

scrapbook paper

banner paper

ruler

tempera paint

yardstick

paintbrushes

pen

pencil

markers

basket

empty container

scissors

shredded paper

cellophane wrap

ribbon

tape

glue

3-ring notebook

clear plastic sleeves

The Band Needs Your Notes!

There's a fun way to express yourself and be part of a group. It's through school music! Decide whether you want to play an instrument or use your voice. Then find a musical group to join at school.

Look through the band or **orchestra** instruments. Test them out. Watch them being played. Do you like the sound? Choose an instrument that you like and start playing.

You may be able to join a group just by signing up. Or you might have to **audition**. This is when you sing or play a song for the director. Then the director decides whether you can join.

There are many different types of music groups to join. Some play classical music and some play marching songs. Some sing pop songs and dance too! Think about the style of music you like. It will help you choose the right group for you.

Make posters or banners to let students know about your music group. Hang them up around school. Soon you'll have new members at your next **rehearsal**!

Music Bazaar

Hold a music bazaar at your school. Students can see instruments up close and learn more about your group. Get a few members of the group together to play. Put instruments on display and invite students to stop by. Be there to answer any questions. If you have flyers, this is a good time to hand them out. It's a great way to get others excited about music!

Band Practice Buzz

Announce your music group practice on a big banner!

What You'll Need

banner paper, pencil, yardstick, tempera paint, paintbrushes, black marker

1 Decide what to say on your banner. How about, "Add Your Voice to The Glee Club!" Or, "Get Loud! Join Band Today!" Make a list of ideas with your group. Vote on the best ideas to use.

2 First sketch the banner in pencil. If you make mistakes, you can erase them!

3 Draw a musical **clef** on the left side. Use the yardstick to draw five straight lines. Start near the clef. Go to the right side of the paper.

4 Write your message on the lines. Make the letters big. Then add when and where your music group meets.

5 It's time to paint! Paint the clef and lines black. Paint the words with bright colors so they really stand out. Add a few musical notes in different colors.

6 When the paint is dry, outline the letters and notes with black marker.

Make Music Together!

Songs are made of many parts. There are parts for different instruments. And there are parts sung by different singers. That's why a music group is like a team.

Being in a music group means that you have to do your part. The group trusts that you will practice on your own. Make a commitment to practice. Set up times each week and follow through. When you sound good, the whole group will sound better.

When you play with your group, communication is important. Listen to the other players. Follow the director's lead. Adjust your playing and be sensitive to the group's sound.

A music group spends long hours practicing. It's important to take a break sometimes. Get together outside of practice. You can make crafts together or play fun games. Try starting with the next activity. Or you can throw a cool party. It will help your group grow closer and help the new members feel not so new!

Dance Party!

A fun way to get to know your teammates is to have a dance party! Ask everyone to bring a CD. Take turns playing each other's music. You'll learn about your team. You'll also have fun dancing to the music!

Musical Match-Up

Learn more about the musicians in your group with this game.

1 Give every group member an index card. Then have them look through the magazines.

2 They should cut out pictures that show the kind of music they like. Maybe it's their favorite band or instrument. They can tape or glue them to their cards.

3 They can add words that **describe** the music they like. Include musicians, instruments, song titles, or music styles.

4 Have everyone write three clues about themselves on the back of their cards. They should help people guess whose card it is. Clues could be their hair color or birthday, or the instrument they play. Make them interesting and fun!

5 Put the index cards in the container. Take turns drawing cards and showing them to the group.

6 Then everyone guesses who made each card. See who is the first one to guess. They can ask for clues if they need help!

Looks to Match Your Moves

Your group's musical style says something about your group. It is one part of your group identity. Find ways to show it. The crowd will notice who's making the music!

When you perform, it's fun to wear a uniform. It makes a good impression for the **audience**. Every member looks like part of a team.

Logos can also make a big impression. A logo is something that can be used on posters, banners, and other printed pieces. It is a symbol that represents a group. Logos can have pictures and words, and the colors are important too.

The following activity will help you create a logo for your music group. Be creative and make it look great. Then use it in different ways to represent your group!

Played by the Funky Notes

Let the crowd know who you are with a cool logo!

What You'll Need
pencil, paper, markers

1 Start with a **brainstorming session** with your group. Ask questions such as *Should our logo have a theme? What words or letters should be in our logo? What picture should be in our logo? What colors should be in our logo?* Write the ideas down.

2 Go through the list with the group. Vote for the best idea for each question and circle it.

3 Now sketch out your idea. Decide what shape you want your logo to fit inside. You could try a music bar or notes! Draw your shape on a piece of paper.

4 Put the picture and words inside the shape. You might need to make several sketches. Move the picture and words around. See what works best. Remember to keep it simple!

5 Show the sketches to your group. What do the other members think? Pick out the logo that everyone likes.

6 Now make a final sketch on a new piece of paper. Make the lines clear and sharp. This will help it look good whether it's printed big or small.

7 Color your logo with markers. Use only a few colors. The colors should look clean and bright.

Play Your Part For Music!

Are you going to perform in another city? That's cool! It costs a lot to travel, though. How will you get the money for the trip? Hold a **fund-raiser** for the music group!

There are many ways to raise money. You can have a garage sale or sell crafts. You can also **raffle** off a musical gift basket. **Brainstorm** ideas with the group and talk with your director. There may be costs to put on your fund-raiser. Include the amount you spend when deciding how much money you need.

Rockin' Raffle

Everyone will want this cool musical basket!

1 Ask people to **donate** items for the gift basket. Go to music and electronics stores. Explain how the **raffle** money will help your group. Ask if they could donate items to put in the gift basket. Tell them you need things such as CDs, T-shirts, headphones, an mp3 player, posters, **concert** tickets. Put shredded paper in the basket. Then arrange the gifts inside. Make sure you can see all the items!

2 Cover the basket and gifts with cellophane. Tie a ribbon at the top. Then put it on display in a safe place at school. Ask the principal or a teacher for ideas.

3 Now you need raffle tickets to sell. Divide a piece of paper into four equal rows. Then draw a vertical line 2 inches (5 cm) from the left side.

4 In the large rectangles, write the details of your **raffle**. What will buyers win? Who are they helping? When will the winner be announced? How will they know if they won? This is also a good place to add your logo! Make each ticket the same.

5 In the small rectangles, make lines for the buyer's information. You will need each buyer's name and a way to contact him or her. It could be a phone number or e-mail address.

6 Make copies and cut out the individual tickets. Give some to each member to sell to their friends and family.

7 Members should give the big part of the tickets to the buyers. They need to keep the small parts. Make sure the buyer fills it out! Put the small tickets in a container.

8 On the day of the drawing, have someone pick the winning ticket from the container. Call or e-mail the winner with the great news!

It's Concert Time!

Performing at **concerts** is the best! It's the result of hours of practice. You need to bring your sheet music, right? Make a cool notebook to carry your music. Show your school spirit!

26

Be sure to carry your music notebook around school. You can also show your school spirit by wearing a group shirt or hat. People will know that you are a part of a music group. If they ask questions, tell them all about your group. It's a chance to get more students **involved** in the fun!

Concerts make practice worth the hard work! Show your school spirit with a positive attitude at a performance. Remember to keep a smile on your face during the show. Also, stay focused and don't goof off. The crowd will love seeing your group perform!

Support Your School!

Here are some fun ways to show your school spirit:

- Perform in the community.

- Wear group shirts.

- Offer to perform at a school **fund-raiser**.

- Talk with other students about your group.

- Make group posters.

- Volunteer together somewhere.

Notes Notebook

The coolest way to
carry your music!

What You'll Need

3-ring notebook, scrapbook paper, pencil, ruler, scissors, ribbon, glue, clear plastic sleeves

1 Choose a piece of scrapbook paper for the background. Lay it face down. Put the notebook on top of it. Trace around the notebook with a pencil.

2 Cut along the traced lines. Then cut 1 inch (2.5 cm) off one side. Glue the paper to the front of the notebook. Line the paper up with the right side of the notebook.

3 Cut a piece of ribbon as long as the notebook is tall. Glue it along the left edge of the paper.

4 Write letters on other pieces of scrapbook paper. You could spell "Music" or your group's name. You could draw musical notes too. Cut out the letters and notes.

5 Set the letters and notes on the notebook. Move them around until it's just the way you want it. Then glue them in place.

6 Wait until the glue dries. Then put the plastic sleeves in the notebook. Fill them up with your sheet music!

Conclusion

What do you love about school music? Is it the cool people you play with? Or do you love learning to read music and playing instruments? It's also fun to perform in front of a crowd. There are so many things that are great about being **involved** with school music.

It is a way to support your school. And you meet people who like the same things as you. It's a great way to make friends and have fun. You get to achieve goals and **participate** in many different activities. This can help you become more **confident** outside of your music group.

School music is one cool way to show your school spirit. But, it is not the only way. Check out the other books in this series. Learn about clubs and groups you can join at your school. Maybe you like to volunteer or play games. Or maybe you think it's fun to learn languages or dance. There will be a club or group that fits your tastes. Take advantage of what your school has to offer. It is a great place to be!

Glossary

audience – a group of people watching a performance.

audition – to try out for a membership in a band or other group.

brainstorm – to come up with a solution by having all members of a group share ideas.

clef – a symbol at the beginning of a line of sheet music.

concert – a musical performance or show.

confident – sure of one's self and one's abilities.

describe – to tell about something with words or pictures.

donate – to give a gift in order to help others.

fund-raise – to raise money for a cause or group. A fund-raiser is an event held to raise funds.

involved – taking part in something.

orchestra – a large group of musicians that play classical music together.

participate – to take part in an activity.

raffle – a way to make money by selling people chances to win a prize.

rehearsal – a meeting where a performance is practiced.

session – a period of time used for a specific purpose or activity.

Web Sites

To learn more about cool school spirit, visit ABDO Publishing Company on the World Wide Web at **www.abdopublishing.com.** Web sites about cool school spirit are featured on our Book Links page. These links are routinely monitored and updated to provide the most current information available.

Index